Contents

GW00566682

Chronology

1122 or 1124: Eleanor's birth

1136: Eleanor becomes Duchess of Aquitaine

1137: Eleanor marries the future King Louis VII

1143: The massacre of Vitry-en-Perthois

1144: Siege of Edessa

1146: Louis VII and Eleanor take the cross

1147: Louis VII and Eleanor set off on their Crusade

1148: In Antioch

1149: Louis VII and Eleanor return to France

1152: Separation of Louis VII and Eleanor, then remarriage between Eleanor and Henry Plantagenet

1154: Eleanor, Queen of England

1157: Birth of Richard the Lionheart

1166: Birth of John Lackland

1169: Eleanor misses the encounter with King Louis VII in Montmirail

1174-1189: Eleanor's captivity

1189: Death of Henry II and coronation of Richard the Lionheart

1199: Death of Richard the Lionheart and coronation of John Lackland

1200: Marriage of Blanche of Castile and Louis VIII of France

1204: Eleanor of Aquitaine dies in Fontevraud

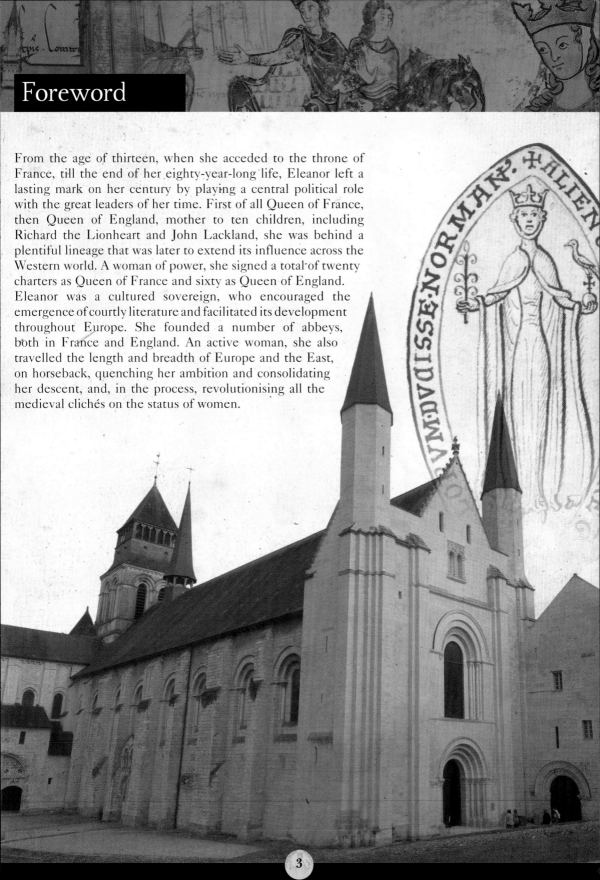

Foreword

From the age of thirteen, when she acceded to the throne of France, till the end of her eighty-year-long life, Eleanor left a lasting mark on her century by playing a central political role with the great leaders of her time. First of all Queen of France, then Queen of England, mother to ten children, including Richard the Lionheart and John Lackland, she was behind a plentiful lineage that was later to extend its influence across the Western world. A woman of power, she signed a total of twenty charters as Queen of France and sixty as Queen of England. Eleanor was a cultured sovereign, who encouraged the emergence of courtly literature and facilitated its development throughout Europe. She founded a number of abbeys, both in France and England. An active woman, she also travelled the length and breadth of Europe and the East, on horseback, quenching her ambition and consolidating her descent, and, in the process, revolutionising all the medieval clichés on the status of women.

Gallia Aquitania

In the early 12th century, the Duke of Aquitaine was an influential figure who had no reason to envy the King of France (whose estate was limited to the present-day Île-de-France region): this powerful lord ruled over a duchy boasting a wealth of crop and fruit farming, along with abundant cattle and horse breeding. The vast forests that thrive within the territory were home to the pigs that were loosed during 'pannage' and, thanks to their walnut trees, offered an abundant source of excellent oil. The salt marshes and vineyards brought financial independence. In major ports, such as La Rochelle and Bordeaux, trading was developed with the rest of Europe, whereas Bayonne, specialised in whale fishing, supplied the entire duchy with fish; the area's demographic growth also escalated, its town fairs drawing merchants from England and even Italy. The duchy's economic prosperity was such that coins were minted in Saintes, Angoulême, Niort and Limoges.

Aquitaine's renown stretched as far as Liège, in Belgium, where Heriger of Lobbes, an abbot who died in 1007, wrote a rather flattering verse in Latin, which translates as, *'Its rivers and streams rich in fish, opulent Aquitaine, sweet as nectar thank to its vineyards dotted about with forests, overflowing with fruit of every kind and endowed with a superabundance of pasture land, filled with gold, silver and other metallic resources, drawing profit from its boats and its* toloneum[1]*...'*

Evangelised very early by its monks, the most famous of whom was Saint Martin of Tours (316-397), Aquitaine was an area of great religious vitality, essentially favoured by its earl-dukes, William V the Great (circa 960-1030) in particular. Abbeys were at the centre of intense economic and cultural activity and were established throughout the territory, contributing towards the development of agriculture in rural areas. The numerous Romanesque churches still bear witness to this religious profusion.

---

1 In the Middle Ages, the toloneum was a tax paid to the lord, at the entry to a port or a bridge, for transporting goods.

Chevet of the Church of Saint-Hilaire in Melle (Deux-Sèvres), considered as one of the finest Romanesque buildings in the Poitevin region.

Recumbent statue of William VII of Aquitaine (1023-1086), Eleanor's great grandfather. Church of Saint-Jean de Montierneuf, in Poitiers (Vienne).

Eleanor's ancestors

From Ranulf I, Count of Poitiers from 854 to 866, to William IX the Troubador, Duke of Aquitaine from 1086 to 1126, who gained renown alongside Godfrey of Bouillon during the first Crusade and who was her grandfather, Eleanor's ancestors included a number of illustrious figures. She also descended from Rollo, who founded Normandy in 911 and whose daughter, Gerloc, married William of Poitiers, also known as Towhead, and was rebaptised Adela or Adèle.

Rollo, one of the six statues that adorn the base of the statue of William the Conqueror on horseback, Falaise (Calvados).

Illumination representing William the Troubador in the *Chansonnier provençal*.

Eleanor's childhood

Eleanor was born in 1122 (or perhaps 1124). Her birthplace remains a mystery; as legend would have it, she was born in the Ombrière Palace, located in the centre of Bordeaux and since disappeared, whilst other sources believe her to have been born in Poitiers. A third theory sees her birthplace in the castle in Belin, a small town to the south of Bordeaux. Dismantled during the French Revolution, all that remains of the castle is the place name *'la butte d'Aliénor'* (Eleanor's mound). In support of this theory, the inhabitants of Belin-Béliet rely on the existence of a charter she had drafted when she was Queen of England. The document afforded them considerable privileges by *'exonerating them from all charges, taxes, duties, all subsidies and servitudes, with no exception, whatever the origin. We therefore wish and we henceforth grant that they benefit in perpetuity, at all times, from the exemptions and liberties that apply to free men.'*

Just like all other girls of her status, Eleanor received excellent instruction. She was taught the works of Ovid, Latin via the Bible, translated by Saint Jerome, music, needlework and *chansons de geste*. So that she could follow her father when hunting, she also learned to ride a horse and to fire a bow. She attended tournaments during which valiant knights broke their spears in her honour.

Daughter to the Count of Poitiers, she was equally at ease with the *langue d'oc* (Occitan language) and the *langue d'oïl* (Oïl language), two dialects, a detail which was to prove of certain importance when she later held her 'Cours d'amour'. Her father, William X, also loved to be entertained by jugglers and singers during the lavish receptions he held in Poitiers, Bordeaux and in his castle in Belin. Memories of her grandfather, William the Troubador, a forerunner of modern poetry, and of the dazzling receptions enlivened by many troubadours, jugglers and musicians who

The royal abbey in Nieul-sur-l'Autise (Vendée).

celebrated courtly love, most probably spurred the young girl's enthusiasm for verbal sparring and lyrical poems. Sumptuousness that she, herself, repeated in the French, then the English royal courts.

Duchess at the age of twelve

The early years of Eleanor's life were saddened by successive bereavements. Eleanor was not even seven when, in 1130, she sadly lost her mother, Aénor of Châtellerault, who was buried in the Abbey of Nieul-sur-l'Autise in Vendée. The same year, her young brother William Aigret died at a very young age; he was the only male heir among her siblings. The duchy was then at risk of 'falling to the distaff'.

Eleanor' fate was totally transformed. In 1136, on the day of her twelfth birthday, the young girl found herself enthroned as the official heir to the duchy by her father, who had gathered all his barons, according to the Aquitaine customs at the time. Before the assembly, his vassals were obliged to bow to her one by one and to swear their loyalty.

Fiancée to the King of the Franks

Yet, William's ambitions for his daughter went much further. Fearing that, after his death, his estate may fall into the hands of avid lords and subsequently be divided, he nurtured other projects; he was as wary of the Count of Anjou as he was of his minor Gascon barons. He consequently envisaged reuniting Aquitaine and the Frankish kingdom by marrying Eleanor with the king's son, hoping to then retire.

On the 9th of April 1137, he sent his faithful companions to Béthisy, the royal residence in Picardy, so they may inform King Louis VI 'the Fat' of his last request: to protect Eleanor, to acknowledge her as his vassal, then to unite her with the heir to the royal throne. The Duke of Aquitaine's emissaries set off to encounter a very sick king, who suffered from dysentery; however, he fully grasped the stakes involved in such a union and granted his consent after consulting his faithful adviser, the abbot Suger of Saint-Denis.

A princely wedding

At the head of a crew of five hundred gentlemen, including Theobald II, Count of Champagne, and Ralph I of Vermandois, Seneschal of France, followed by a multitude of cattle-drawn carts filled with gifts, young prince Louis rode to Bordeaux to meet with Eleanor, accompanied by Suger. Their engagement was celebrated, then their marriage, on Sunday 25th of July 1137, in the Cathedral of Saint Andrew in Bordeaux.

The grand festivities lasted several days, with much merrymaking to the sound of flutes, viols, zithers and tambourines. The newly-weds were very young: Eleanor had not yet reached the age of thirteen. Louis was barely seventeen. A few days later, Prince Louis, his court, Eleanor and her suite headed for Limoges, then Poitiers, so that Louis could celebrate his union once more and receive the ducal crown. However, the crown did not mean the duchy, and Eleanor continued to exercise her prerogative as Duchess of Aquitaine. Throughout their journey, the festivities and receptions continued. Eleanor brought along her sister, Petronilla, also known as Alix.

It was after the ceremony – which was as solemn as it was sumptuous – in the Cathedral of Saint Peter in Poitiers, that Prince Louis was proclaimed Duke of Aquitaine. As he approached the town of Poitiers, a bereaved messenger bowed before him and announced the death of his father Louis VI, *'The king is dead, long live the king!'* Louis the Young, whom his father had associated with the kingdom six years previously – when he was still a child – by having him crowned king in Reims by Pope Innocent II, became the *de facto* King of the Franks, under the name of Louis VII.

Illumination representing Louis VII and Eleanor's wedding in the *Grandes Chroniques de France*.

The young king left his equally young wife under the protection of the Bishop of Chartres, putting an end to the festivities so that he could hurry to Paris and take the throne. In doing so, he avoided any rebellion against the new royal power. The following Christmas, Louis was once more crowned King of the Franks, this time in the Cathedral of Saint Stephen of Bourges. Eleanor was also crowned queen.

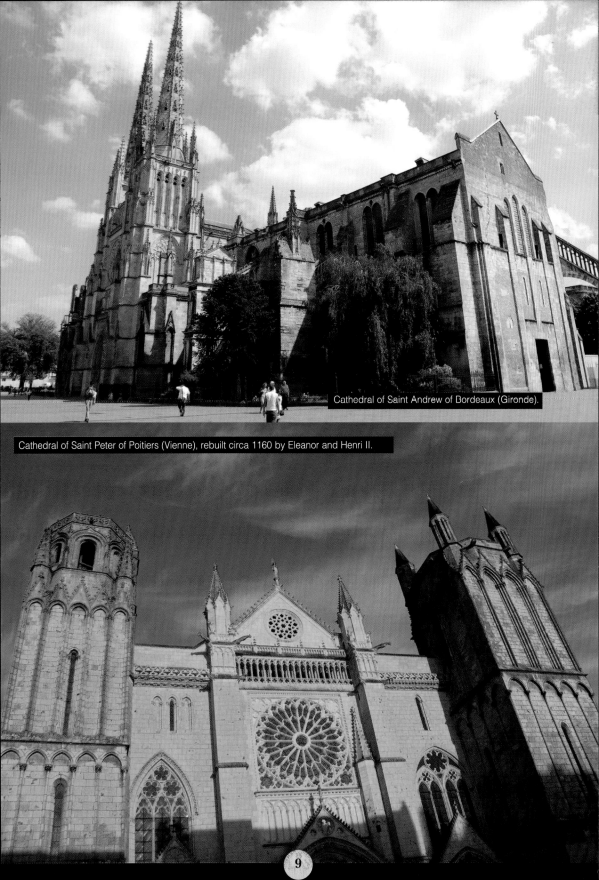

Cathedral of Saint Andrew of Bordeaux (Gironde).

Cathedral of Saint Peter of Poitiers (Vienne), rebuilt circa 1160 by Eleanor and Henri II.

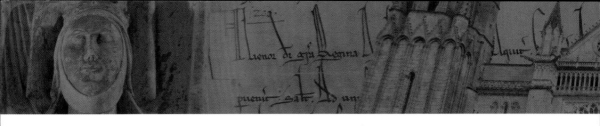

Louis VII, 'the Young', the unexpected King of the Franks

The son of Louis VI 'the Fat' and of Adelaide of Savoy was not destined to govern but to live a monastic career. Yet, an unfortunate accident was to change his plans. On the 13th of October 1131, Philip, the crown prince, was riding through the streets of Paris with other young horsemen. Suddenly, a pig literally threw itself at the horse's legs, causing the animal to fall, and Philip with it.

Philip died a few hours later. *'Porcus diabolicus'*, Suger later exclaimed in his *Chroniques de France*. The new king did not have his father's political influence. During his reign, the latter had succeeded in consolidating his frontiers from William the Conqueror's ambitious heirs – who had, in turn, become Kings of England – and in stabilising his kingdom and rendering France a prosperous country.

In the early days of his reign, Louis VII was to face several rebellions, stirred up by noblemen wishing to challenge his authority. The inhabitants of Aquitaine, in turn, had trouble accepting the king's stranglehold on the land that once belonged to the deceased Duke William X. Hence, in 1138, the burghers from Poitiers decided to transform their town into a Medieval commune[1]. King Louis VII and his army launched an assault on the town, forcing its inhabitants to surrender. Strict repression ensued, and it was only thanks to Suger's intervention that the rebels' children were not taken hostage. Suger's role in the story was not to the liking of Eleanor, who duly informed the king. From then on, the royal couple called far less frequently on the abbot, who consequently preferred to retire to his abbey in Saint Denis, depriving the king of his precious counsel.

---

1 In feudal times, the king could grant the burghers of a town with a charter, a privilege which enabled them to goern their town – which became a 'commune' – independently. In the case of Poitiers, the burghers transformed their town into a commune without consulting the king.

Louis VII, 'the Young', represented in the *Recueil des Rois de France*, by Jean du Tillet, 15th century.

Illumination illustrating Louis VII's coronation in the *Grandes Chroniques de France*.

Eleanor's life at the royal court

Eleanor's early days at the royal court proved difficult. She was totally different from Louis: the young woman, whose youth had been instructive and sophisticated, had developed her own, strong personality; the king was, in contrast, rather quiet, living an austere life dedicated to devotion. *'I have married a monk,'* Eleanor was to say of him. At the time, the king's palace occupied a large share of the Île de la Cité in Paris, which had been surrounded by ramparts since the Norman invasions in the 9th and 10th centuries. Paris was, as yet, a small market town surrounded by forests and with a population of just a few thousand.

It was of no comparison to the sumptuous properties Eleanor had become familiar with in Poitiers and Bordeaux. As soon as she took up residence, Eleanor found herself faced with hostility from the queen mother, Adelaide of Savoy, who kept a jealous watch on her son's crown. The young sovereign, who had hitherto bathed in her southern culture,

Crystal vase depicting Eleanor, brought back from the Crusades by William the Troubador and offered as a gift to Suger.

struggled greatly to accustom herself with the strict rules of the court, where intrigues of all sorts were rife. Eleanor had maintained the taste for luxury she had nurtured in her father's court. Nothing was too beautiful for the young queen, who ordered sumptuous tapestries to adorn the walls of the ceremonial room and her apartments. She also had merchants bring in the most sophisticated of oriental perfumes. Furthermore, Eleanor invited troubadours to play in the court. Considered as scandalous practice, this was only to foster further jealousy from the king. The poet Marcabru was duly dismissed, due to the love poems he wrote for his queen.

Illumination depicting Marcabru in the *Chansonnier Provençal*. He was born in Auvillar (Tarn-et-Garonne).

The warfaring adventures of the young royal couple

The young queen, determined to assert her power over her Duchy of Aquitaine, sent her husband off on a number of warfaring expeditions to submit his vassals to his royal authority. William of Lezay, the lord of Talmont, who had subtilised the Duke of Aquitaine's white falcons, was to pay the price of such expeditions. Further scandal came from the presence at the royal court of Eleanor's young sister Petronilla, who had developed a particular fondness for the Seneschal of France, Ralph of Vermandois. The latter hoped to marry her. However, to do so, he would need to repudiate his first wife, Eleanor of Blois, on the grounds of consanguinity. Under Eleanor's influence, he gained support from Louis VII. However, the repudiated spouse's brother, Thibaut of Blois, Count of Champagne, would have none of it and appealed to Pope

Innocent II. Consequently, in 1143, Louis VII decided to take over the land belonging to the Count of Champagne and besieged the small town of Vitry-en-Perthois, where the inhabitants sought refuge inside the church. Irreparable tragedy ensued when the king's soldiers set fire to the building, causing the death of over 1,300 innocent people. As the indirect author of these acts of violence, Eleanor's prestige took a blow, both among the royal court and the ecclesiastic authorities. The event had a major consequence on the Kingdom of France, leading to the Pope's interdiction, which deprived the country of the right to celebrate any religious ceremony whatsoever. Yet, the king's soldiers continued their incursions in Champagne until September, plunging the region into terror and desolation.

The penitent king

'*Given the violence that you continue to exert, I am beginning to repent from always having attributed your errors to the inexperience of youth... Following advice inspired by the Demon, you have returned to committing the ill deeds you once repented from causing and have opened wounds that were once healed... I will cry out that you are multiplying murders, fires, church destruction, that you are chasing the poor from their homes, that you are committing these deeds with abductors and brigands... Be warned, you will not remain unpunished for very long... I speak harshly to you, but I fear that even harsher chastisement awaits you...*' When a monk named Bernard of Clairvaux spoke to his king in such terms, his allusion to the harmful influence his wife Eleanor exerted on him was but thinly veiled. Personified by Bernard, the entire Church condemned these seven calamitous years for the Kingdom of France.

These alarming works had somewhat shaken the king, who felt increasing remorse. He set to praying incessantly, to fasting and to seeking penitence. The festive evenings enlivened by the troubadours were no more! And when, on the 11th of June 1144, the king accepted Suger's invitation to attend the inauguration of the brand new choir in the abbey-church of Saint Denis, he did so donning the appropriate penitent's attire – a frieze robe and sandals – and walking humbly towards the church entrance. A striking contrast with the queen's attire, magnificently trimmed with diamonds and a dazzling silk dress adorned with motifs made of precious stones and gold and silver yarn. The crowd that flocked in masses alongside the royal cortège was stunned by the scene. Louis VII relentlessly strove to atone for his faults. He therefore decided to make a pilgrimage to Jerusalem, which he hoped would appease his conscience. Before leaving, he withdrew his soldiers from Champagne and made peace with Count Thibaut.

Detail of the stained-glass window of the Childhood of Christ, representing the Abbot Suger, Basilica of Saint Denis.

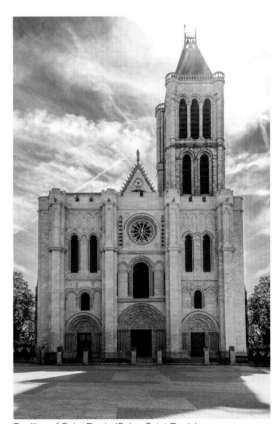

Basilica of Saint Denis (Seine-Saint-Denis).

1144: the siege of Edessa and its consequences

Concurrent events in the Holy Land were to transform his pilgrimage into a warfaring expedition. Upon the death of Fulk IV, Count of Anjou, who had to date reigned over Jerusalem, his son being too young to do so, the Crusader states were plunged into chaos, advantage of which was taken by Imad ad-Din Zengi, the emir of Mosul (today located in Iraq). On the 23rd of December 1144, after a four-week siege, his soldiers took control of the county of Edessa. The consequences were dramatic for the Christian populations who suffered fifteen thousand dead. The town was ransacked, churches and several monasteries were destroyed. The siege of Edessa was to mark the beginning of a new Islamic conquest.

It was only in February the following year that the news reached Rome. The new Pope sent his emissaries to meet with the Frankish king, asking him to lead an expedition aimed at recovering the lost holy sites. The king replied favourably to the Pope's request and decided to announce to the court he held in Bourges, during the 'crowned festivities' for Christmas 1145, his commitment to offering his support to the Church of the East. The noblemen he gathered around him showed their reluctance, but Louis VII did not for as much give up on his crusading project. Meanwhile, the same year, Eleanor gave birth to a daughter, Marie.

Miniature depicting Louis VII's departure for the Crusades, in the *Grandes Chroniques de France*.

1146: 'The favourable time has now come'

A few months later, on the 31st of March 1146, Easter Sunday, all of France's nobility was invited to Vézelay. Noblemen and yokels alike flocked before the platform installed on the hillside to listen to the monk of Clairvaux preach. Bernard began his speech by reading the Papal bull issued three weeks previously and urged the Frankish lords to engage. Galvanised by the future saint's words, they all enthusiastically accepted his appeal, following Louis VII's example. Louis received a red cross which Bernard attached to his chest; then followed the king's brothers, the Count of Flanders, Raymond, Count of Toulouse, Thibaut II, Count of Champagne – once one of the king's staunch adversaries. The pride of the French aristocracy all wanted to receive the cross, followed by the prelates. In the wildest of delirium, the crowd also rushed forward to receive the precious red fabric cross.

Louis VII taking the cross at Vézelay, 15th century miniature, *Passages faiz oultre mer par les François contre les Turcqs et autres Sarrazins et Mores oultre marins*, Sébastien Mamerot, circa 1473-1474.

12th May 1147:
en route for the Holy Land

During the council held in Étampes on the 16th of February 1147, Louis VII made arrangements before his departure and appointed Suger as regent of his kingdom during his absence. He also needed to levy taxes to fund his expedition costs and to organise his army. In doing so, he provided for the numerous carts filled with drink and foodstuffs, but also for the necessary equipment for his travels: tent rolls, iron chests filled with gold coins, an impressive wardrobe, furs, rugs, cooking equipment, etc. All of these goods were drawn by strong, sturdy horses. He also needed to guarantee his diplomatic alliances: after lengthy negotiations, Roger II of Sicily agreed to offer refuge to the French soldiers and to the king's ships and supplies.

Raymond of Poitiers welcoming Louis VII to Antioch, after an illumination by Jean Colombe, *Passages faiz oultre mer par les François contre les Turcqs et autres Sarrazins et Mores oultre marins*, Sébastien Mamerot, circa 1473-1474.

A crusader by the name of Eleanor

King Louis was not the only member of the royal family to engage in the Crusade. Eleanor decided to accompany him. She most likely was thinking of her grandfather William the Troubador's glorious past, as a hero of the First Crusade. With her, a number of highly noble ladies also headed for the Holy Land, accompanied by their chambermaids and ladies-in-waiting. Queen Eleanor had succeeded in convincing a great share of Gascony's and Poitiers' nobility to follow her on the Crusade and large numbers of Aquitaine's lords and ladies followed in the footsteps of their queen and duchess. Before she left, Eleanor visited all her duchy's abbeys to gather funds, in exchange for substantial gifts. The journey, which was slowed down by the queen's impressive cortège, was to last five months, encountering difficulties of all sorts, given the great number of pilgrims marching behind the king and the queen. Supplies were late to be delivered to the inhabitants of the lands they travelled through, despite the large sums brought in by Suger. In Constantinople, the royal couple and its suite were welcomed by the Emperor Manuel Komnenos, who had prepared a grand reception for them. The banquet he offered abounded with delicious dishes. Eleanor, always willing to test novel things, discovered the finest of foods, seasoned with the rarest of spices, such as coriander and cumin. Caviar and artichokes, as yet unknown in France in the 12th century, accompanied with heady Greek wines, delighted the Emperor's guests.

1148: in Antioch

After three weeks of grand festivities, punctuated by tournaments and hunting trips, Louis VII decided to leave Constantinople and travel to Nicaea to join forces with the German King Conrad III and his army, also engaged in the Crusade. There, he found a routed army of barely a few thousand scrawny and weak soldiers. The military campaign, which proved more costly than planned, was to increasingly weaken the State funds, all the more so since Conrad's troops also needed to be provided for and the rest of the German army reorganised. When he reached Attalea (Antalya in present-day Turkey) on the 19th of January 1148, Louis boarded part of his elite horsemen onto ships provided by the emperor Manuel, leaving other healthy men to march to Tarsus, escorted by Byzantines.

With difficulty, the French army was reunited in Antioch in the spring of 1148 and the royal couple was welcomed with great pomp by the town's reigning prince, Raymond of Poitiers. Eleanor, who was in fact Raymond's niece, was delighted – after several months challenging disloyal soldiers – to find herself amidst her uncle's court, in an atmosphere similar to the one she had cherished so in her younger years by her father, William of Aquitaine's side: verbal sparring in Occitan language, the rarest of dishes served by obliging valets, troubadours and, of course, all the charm of the East: mild evenings, long walks amidst the olive trees... Very quickly, the close complicity shared by Raymond and his niece made the king feel somewhat excluded. The ten days Eleanor spent in Antioch were an enchantment to the young queen. It was even murmured amidst the king's circle that Eleanor may have succumbed to the charms of her uncle, *'of finer body and more handsome than any of his companions'* according to the chroniclers. A dispute broke out between Louis VII and Raymond.

The latter envisaged recapturing Edessa in order to ensure his principality's safety, whilst the King of the Franks proclaimed his wishes to leave Antioch as soon as possible to pray at the Holy Sepulchre. Eleanor sided with her uncle, clearly stating her desire to remain in Antioch with her vassals. For Louis, it was the ultimate affront and he threatened to exert his matrimonial rights to force the queen to see reason. In vain, as Eleanor retorted that their marriage was spoiled by consanguinity. Nevertheless, tired of resisting and under duress, Eleanor was to follow her husband, who seemed oblivious to the grave consequences this forced departure would have on the couple's future.

Expedition then fiasco

The pursuit of this second crusade proved to be calamitous for the king, who was defeated at the gates of Damascus after a four-day siege. His dreams of conquest were over. Chaos and retreat were rife: the German King Conrad decided to withdraw, leaving Louis VII and his army alone in Jerusalem. He was then informed of Raymond of Poitiers' further defeat at the Battle of Inab, after which he was beheaded by soldiers from the Emir of Aleppo's army. After spending a few months in holy places, Louis VII, called home by Suger, finally resigned himself to return to France. Eleanor, who did not travel aboard the same boat as the king, was captured by Turks. Thanks to negotiations engaged by the Normans of Sicily, the queen was freed and joined Louis VII three weeks later. The outcome of this second crusade was experienced as a great failure for Christianity itself: thousands of horsemen killed on the battlefield, and not one single victory against their enemies who had, on the contrary, reinforced their positions. The crusade had only contributed towards further chaos in the region.

Separation made public

The royal couple returned to French soil separately. Although common practice during crossings that were deemed perilous, this particular separation symbolised the end of a union. Eleanor appeared determined to request the annulment of her marriage on the grounds of consanguinity, despite intervention by the Pope in an attempt to reconcile the royal spouses. Their reconciliation was short-lived...

Eleanor's repudiation, in the *Grandes Chroniques de France*.

Barely the time to conceive their second child, Alix, born in 1151 – another girl! This was only to exacerbate the king's resentment for his wife. Yet, Louis VII was far from imagining the humiliation Eleanor was secretly preparing. In March 1152, in Beaugency, their marriage bond, which had lasted for fifteen years, was officially broken by a synod of bishops on the grounds of kinship, upon Eleanor's personal request. The bishops based their decision on the fact that Adelaide of Aquitaine (circa 945-1004), daughter of William Towhead, had married the King Hugh Capet, who was one of Louis VII's direct ancestors, around the year 968. Eleanor, who had recovered her titles of Countess of Poitiers and Duchess of Aquitaine, left the French royal court and headed for Poitiers, leaving – as was the custom at the time – her two daughters with their father who, when the time came, would ably introduce them to appropriate suitors.

The origins of a failed union

There were many reasons behind this separation. First of all, they stemmed from the profound discord between Louis VII and Eleanor. The journey to the East had revived a certain taste for the life she had once known during her childhood years, the memories of which she had pushed aside, from marital duty, when she settled in Paris. The young woman, who had grown up amidst an educated and luxurious court, found it increasingly difficult to accept her husband's devout attitude and became bored in his company. The second reason was of a political nature. As soon as he returned to France, the king drew closer to Suger and fully intended to reign alone, without – as he had done previously – consulting the queen. Yet, in doing so, he underestimated Eleanor's strength of character and she readily reminded him, whenever the slightest opportunity arose, that she was the duchess of an estate

that was at least as important as the Capetian's. If truth be told, it would appear that Eleanor had carefully prepared the aftermath of their separation. For France's richest heiress, it was simply impossible to imagine marrying any old local squire. She needed to find a spouse who was worthy of her political ambitions. Her choice went to Henry Plantagenet, a handsome and powerful lord who had just inherited the estate that had belonged to his recently deceased father, Geoffrey Plantagenet. Duke of Normandy, Count of Anjou and of Maine, Henry was the son of Empress Matilda and the grandson of the King of England, Henry I Beauclerc. He was, therefore, a direct descendent of William the Conqueror, founder of the English dynasty. He was logically in line to replace his mother's cousin, the King Stephen of Blois, whose calamitous reign had wreaked havoc across England and whose son and heir apparent, Eustace, had just passed away. It was a highly political union, but also a love match for these two young newly-weds, with a great yearning for glory and power. Through their marriage, the Plantagenet estate stretched from the Channel coast to the Pyrenean Mountains. The dismal evenings spent at the French court with an austere king were a thing of the past.

One can easily suppose that the secret dealings between the future spouses had already begun during Henry Plantagenet's stay at the court, when Eleanor was still in the midst of 'divorce proceedings'.

Divorce in the Middle Ages

Divorce did not officially exist in the 12th century. However, the Church could grant that a couple separate based on certain specific criteria:
- repudiation of the wife for serious misdeed (adultery);
- repudiation of the wife for sterility;
- annulment of the marriage on the grounds of consanguinity between husband and wife.

In the case of Eleanor and Louis VII, the third reason formed the basis of the dissolution of their marriage.

18th May 1152: a new marriage

Eleanor and Henry Plantagenet's wedding was celebrated on the 18th of May 1152 in the Cathedral of Saint Peter of Poitiers, just a few weeks after her separation with Louis VII. The announcement of the event, even if it was celebrated without pomp and circumstance, was a terrible blow to King Louis' court. Eleanor had inflicted outright humiliation on her ex-husband, embarrassing him even more so by countering the customary feudal rules by marrying one of the king's vassals without asking his permission. Furthermore, over and above her existing titles of Countess of Poitiers and Duchess of Aquitaine, Eleanor could now add Countess of Anjou and Duchess of Normandy.

Eleanor and Henry II of England, depicted on the Crucifixion window in the Cathedral of Saint Peter of Poitiers.

Henri Plantagenet, King of England

Henry Plantagenet, born in Le Mans on the 5th of March 1133, was the son of Geoffrey Plantagenet. A stock and sturdy redhead, he was said to spend most of his time on horseback. He had a strong personality, boasting both charm and culture. He was perfectly familiar with the laws of his country and had an excellent command of both Latin and French. As the worthy son of Empress Matilda, an ambitious woman who, her whole life over, had claimed the throne of England, Henry incessantly waged war in attempts to take the throne occupied by Stephen of Blois.

Things changed dramatically, and fast, when Stephen lost his son Eustace. The King of England had no choice but to promise the throne to Henry Plantagenet by signing, on the 6th of November 1153, the Treaty of Wallingford, which brought an end to years of unrest. When they learned of King Stephen's death on the 5th of October 1154, during their stay in Rouen, Henry and Eleanor – who was expecting their second child – set off to cross the English Channel from Barfleur, taking their one year-old son William with them; they were followed by a striking parade of armed men who escorted a horde of barons and ecclesiastics. After landing in Southampton, the cortège headed first of all for Winchester, before travelling to London, where it was soon joined by several horsemen who had boarded in other Norman ports. Throughout their journey, the mere sight of the young couple spurred ovations and cries of joy from the population. Exhausted by years of civil war, their hopes were now set on Henry Plantagenet to bring newfound peace to the nation.

Geoffrey Plantagenet's copper and enamel tombstone, 12th century, Carré Plantagenêt, Le Mans museum of archaeology and history (Sarthe). It adorned the grave of Geoffrey Plantagenet, buried in Le Mans Cathedral (Sarthe), which was desecrated during the Wars of Religion in 1562. On the shield, one can distinguish five leopards, three of which were adopted by his grandson, Richard the Lionheart, to adorn his standard. Today, two of these leopards are represented 'de gueule' (on a red background) on the Normandy flag, and one on the Guyenne flag.

19th December 1154: Eleanor's coronation

Following a highly specific ritual, the official coronation ceremony took place in London on the 19th of December 1154, in Westminster Cathedral. Henry was seated on a throne to the right of the choir, whereas Eleanor faced him on another throne to the left of the choir. All the English aristocrats were there of course, but the greatest of lords from both Normandy, Anjou, Aquitaine and Poitou were also invited to attend the ceremony. Henry of Anjou received the royal crown from Theobald of Bec, the Archbishop of Canterbury, to become Henry II; then it was Eleanor's turn to be crowned.

Westminster Abbey, London (Great Britain).

THE EMPIRE OF
THE ANGEVINS

Scale of Stat. Miles

London: Macmillan & Cº

'The Plantagenet Empire'

Through his marriage with Eleanor, Henry II found himself master of an immense territory that now included England, Normandy, Maine, Anjou, Poitou and Aquitaine... as far as the Pyrenean foothills. An estate that was later to be extended to include Brittany and the eastern part of Ireland. It was such a vast territory that historians refer to it as the 'Plantagenet Empire', a genuine threat to the Kingdom of France. Louis VII was to fully grasp, but only later alas, the terrible political error he had made in repudiating Eleanor. Henry, a vassal to the King of the Franks, was to reign for over thirty years over his vast estate. This situation, which was intolerable for Louis VII, was later to be a source of conflict between his son Philip Augustus and Henry's successors, Richard the Lionheart and John Lackland.

The Plantagenet estate is indicated in orange, the Kingdom of France in light green. Extract from the book by John Richard Green *A Short History of the English People*, 1895.

1153-1166: childbirth repeated

Eleanor, who had failed to offer Louis VII a male heir, later gave birth to five sons and three daughters, for a grand total of ten pregnancies. Her youngest child, John, was born in 1166 when Eleanor was aged over forty. Yet, her successive pregnancies did not prevent her from following Henry on his many travels, hence demonstrating the role she intended to assume as Queen of England. As was custom at the time, nannies, such as Hodierne and Agathe, looked after educating the children when they were young. They were later entrusted to private tutors who taught them Latin and literature – men of the Church, such as Thomas Becket. Over and above this education, boys also learned how to wage war, thanks to instruction from the master of arms, William Marshal. The couple's youngest two children, Joan and John, were entrusted to monks and cloistered nuns from the Abbey of Fontevraud in Anjou.

Ruins of Domfront Castle (Orne) where, in 1161, Eleanor and Henry II's daughter, also named Eleanor, was baptised. She became Queen of Castile.

Coronation of Henry the Lion and his wife Matilda, Henry the Lion's evangelistary.

Statue of Henry the Lion in Brunswick (Germany).

Eleanor did not for as much lose interest in her children's future. She travelled to Normandy, on the occasion of the court held there by Henry early 1160, to pay a visit to their daughter Matilda, who had been placed in a convent. When the girl's father decided she should marry the Duke of Saxony in September 1167, Eleanor personally reunited the sumptuous gifts for the future couple. No less than three ships were requisitioned to cross the English Channel with the numerous courtiers and gifts that comprised the young girl's dowry. Accompanied by her mother, the young princess was introduced to Henry the Lion, whom she was to marry in Minden Cathedral in Lower Saxony. The wedding, held in Brunswick Castle, lasted three days. Eleanor, who – as we know – had quite a penchant for grand and sumptuous receptions, must have particularly appreciated the festivities.

1152-1174: Eleanor, a governing queen

As she had done when she was Queen of France, Eleanor intended to fully accomplish her role as a sovereign. She was perfectly able to assist Henry II, to whom she offered astute advice when important decisions were to be made. The young king was highly active and full of energy, which was much to the liking of Eleanor who had suffered from boredom when in Louis' court. When Henry travelled to Normandy, Eleanor signed acts on his behalf, readily dispensing justice and granting privileges to her subjects whenever the opportunity arose. For example, she acted in favour of the Reading monks, who complained of having been unjustly despoiled of their land.

She could also be seen sitting on the Christmas Courts that were held each year in a different residence on either shore of the Channel: in Westminster of course, but also in Falaise, Bayeux, Cherbourg, Domfront, Limoges and Bordeaux. Reuniting all the members of the aristocracy, these courts were highly important and were an excellent pretext for festivities and hunting parties.

Similarly, when the king was busy in England, Eleanor looked after his estates in Normandy and Anjou. She attended sessions at the Exchequer, a genuine economic court and a financial windfall for maintaining the kingdom. Eleanor equally cherished her status as a sovereign and as a woman, enjoying an extremely fulfilling role as Queen of England. Her multiple activities did not prevent her from lavishing in luxury, buying many clothes, precious stones and crockery she had gilded. From her travels to Constantinople, Eleanor had developed a taste for the subtlest of perfumes and the rarest of spices of her time, readily having cumin, cinnamon, ginger and pepper brought in from the East, all of them regularly unloaded in the port of Bordeaux to adorn the royal tables during grand high society receptions.

Eleanor's seal.

Stained glass window in the Town Hall in Poitiers (Vienne), representing Eleanor before the aldermen, Steinhel, 1874.

Falaise Castle
(Calvados):
the Small Keep.

Falaise Castle:
residential floor of
the Small Keep.

Henry II, the unfaithful

Henry II eventually grew tired of a wife who was continuously expecting and older than himself. He ceased to conceal his relationship with Rosamund Clifford, which was to arouse Eleanor's jealousy. Two sons were born from this adulterous relationship; Geoffrey, future Archbishop of York and William Longsword. The royal couple's discord was finally made public on the 6th of January 1169, when Henry was welcomed by the King of France to Montmirail Castle. During a solemn ceremony, he implored Louis VII for 'protection' for his three sons, Henry, Geoffrey and Richard. Based on political events concerning the quarrel between Henry and Thomas Becket, the Archbishop of Canterbury – who had sought refuge with the Court of France – it was also decided that Richard would marry Alys of France.

Eleanor's absence during the encounter in Montmirail failed to escape anyone. Perhaps she had deemed inappropriate to meet with he who had been her husband for fifteen years; perhaps – and more probably – there was a different and far more secret reason: the King of England's unfaithfulness to Eleanor.

Henceforth, Eleanor made less frequent journeys to England, preferring Poitiers, where she had her son Richard named Duke of Aquitaine, in June 1172, without consulting the king.

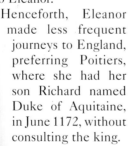

Montmirail Castle (Sarthe).

The Cours d'amour of the 'Eagle'

Poitiers became Eleanor's favourite residence. She was seen there governing and making decisions concerning the management of her duchy. She gathered together her children, including her daughter Marie of Champagne, born from her marriage with Louis VII of France. Her preference appeared to go to Richard. The capital of the Poitou region soon became the cultural centre of the Plantagenet kingdom and was home to Chrétien de Troyes, who wrote *Lancelot*, and to the poets Bernard de Ventadour and Bertran de Born, among others. They all rivalled in poetic prowess in Occitan language or wrote books on chivalry. Richard, who had inherited his mother's taste for poetry, was well catered for, as was his half-sister Marie. Thanks to Eleanor's daughters, an entire literary movement then developed and stretched across Europe, from Champagne to Sicily, from Saxony to England, from Aquitaine to Castile. For the poets, she who was given the epithet of 'Eagle' by Guernes de Pont-Sainte-Maxence, very prettily bore the name of *alie* (eagle) and *or* (gold). '*Honest, gentle and loyal, by whom the king shall be happy, gracious beauty, of fine body, I who was nothing, she has made me rich.*' (Bernard de Ventadour). However, Eleanor did not forget her obligations as Queen of England. As such, she made appearances, accompanying Henry, during the Christmas Courts in Bur (the present-day village of Noron-la-Poterie, in Calvados) in 1170 and in Chinon in 1172.

Der Von Kürenberg (German troubadour) speaking with Eleanor, Große Heidelberger Liederhandschrift.

Eleanor being sent into captivity, fresco, St. Radegonde Chapel.

1174-1189: Eleanor's captivity

The discord between Eleanor and Henry was made public in 1173, during the rebellions initiated by Princes Henry, Geoffrey and Richard against their father, who had had the Archbishop Thomas Becket assassinated in Canterbury Cathedral. The three princes were impatient to reign over their respective territories, as Henry had stated in the will he had dictated in 1170. Their rebellion was largely encouraged by Eleanor and supported by Louis VII. This was too much for Henry, who had the queen captured in the Touraine region. Then began a long period of fifteen years of captivity, firstly in Chinon, then in England. As a recluse, Eleanor nevertheless received occasional visits from her daughter Marie, with whom she maintained close family ties. However, this long period of house arrest was also a time for bereavement, for news of the death of her son Henry the Young King, due to dysentery, came to Eleanor in 1183. Three years later, her other son, Geoffrey, who had taken refuge with the Court of France, was killed in Paris during a jousting tournament.

Henry, who had stayed alone in England, sensed the void engulfing him. His beautiful Rosamund also died. Richard, who was the official heir to the English throne, decided to stay in France in the company of the young King Philip Augustus, to whom he paid homage. Henry was left with the exclusive support of his youngest son, John, to whom he had secretly promised the throne. Yet, to succeed his father, he would need to undertake a military campaign against his brother Richard, who had allied with Louis VII. Hostilities were resumed early 1189. The King of England led his very last battle in Chinon, this time facing death. He breathed his last breath on the 6th of July 1189, a date that marked Eleanor's imminent release. She was aged around sixty-five.

St. Radegonde Chapel,
Chinon (Indre-et-Loire).

Serving Richard the Lionheart

As soon as she was released, Eleanor relentlessly strove to assert her authority. She was seen riding from town to town, granting privileges, founding abbeys and hospitals, controlling justice made by the sheriffs and the kingdom's finances, restoring order and having alms given to the poor. But she was more particularly seen preparing for her son Richard's coronation. The extravagant celebrations around the coronation ceremony reminded Eleanor of her bygone years. Barely had he received the crown when Richard decided to set off on a Crusade to liberate the Holy Sepulchre in Jerusalem. He entrusted his kingdom's regency to his mother. Eleanor could well have contented herself with managing the kingdom during Richard's absence.

Yet, her resolute desire to see the new king wed, and to offer a new heir to the throne, decided otherwise. She made an incredible journey on horseback from London to Messina, in Sicily, in the company of Berengaria, the daughter of King Sancho VI of Navarre, whom she had chosen for Richard (the hand of Louis VII's daughter, Alys of France, had been promised to Richard; however, the young princess was but a child when she was raped by Henry II and, therefore, could no longer become Richard's wife, all the more so since she had given birth to a child). Eleanor's trip to Messina was also the opportunity for renewed contact with her daughter Joan, the widow of the King of Sicily. Once she had accomplished her maternal duty, she was keen to return as quickly as possible to England, a kingdom now threatened by her

Coronatio. illustris reg. anglorum Ricardi.

youngest son John's thirst for power. He had rumours of the king's death spread, in order to take over the regency until such times as Richard the Lionheart returned from the Crusade. A return which proved to be eventful. On his way back from the Holy Land, Richard was taken prisoner by the Holy Roman Emperor Henry VI. Once more, Eleanor could be seen going to great efforts across the kingdom, levying taxes to pay the ransom, fearing that the crown may fall into the hands of John Lackland, whom she deemed incapable of governing. Once she had finally reunited sufficient treasures, Eleanor led the convoy that crossed the English Channel and headed for Mainz, in German territory, and brought her triumphant son back to England, where he would be crowned once more. The festivities continued as far as Normandy, where Richard and his mother were welcomed by a fervent crowd.

Richard's coronation, Cotton Manuscripts, Sir Robert Bruce Cotton collection.

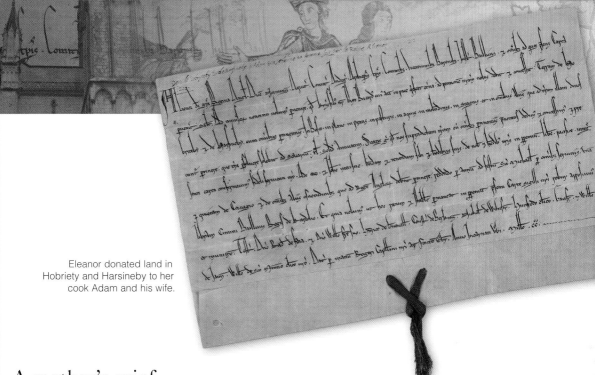

Eleanor donated land in Hobriety and Harsineby to her cook Adam and his wife.

A mother's grief

Exhausted by a life of combat, Eleanor retired to her dear Abbey of Fontevraud, the wealth of which had benefited from her contributions. She desired to spend her last days in rest and prayer. It was during this retreat that she learned that her dearest son Richard had been mortally wounded by a crossbow arrow during a warfaring expedition in Limousin in 1199. She personally brought his body back to the abbey to have him buried alongside his father, Henry II. Upon the death of Richard *'her very dear sire'*, all that Eleanor had so dearly striven to achieve to offer the Plantagenet kingdom its great splendour, collapsed. With a heavy heart, she resigned herself to allowing her last son, John, take the English throne, along with the duchies of Normandy, Aquitaine and Poitou. Eleanor's grief was revived once more when, five months later, her daughter Joan, who had remarried with the Count of Toulouse, died during childbirth. Despite these unfortunate events, the old queen decided to make one last tour of Aquitaine. Much to her satisfaction, she found her duchy as prosperous as ever. A few months later, she attended the court of King Philip Augustus, to whom she paid homage for her land.

1199-1200: Eleanor's last cavalcade

Of the children she had had with her husband Henry II, only John Lackland – now king – and Eleanor, who had married Alfonso VIII of Castile, remained. Hence, the ageing queen began to nurture hopes of organising a union between one of her granddaughters with Louis, the crown Prince of France. Once more, Eleanor had her palfrey saddled and, in the midst of the winter, rode across Aquitaine on her way to Burgos, in Castile, where Alfonso VIII and his family resided. She chose her granddaughter Blanca. Later known as Blanche of Castile, the young girl was brought to Normandy by her grandmother, where she married the future King Louis VIII and, in doing so, brought short-lived peace between France and England.

Detail of the recumbent statue of Eleanor of Aquitaine, book in hand, evoking her intellectual past, Abbey of Fontevraud (Maine-et-Loire).

Fontevraud, necropolis to the Plantagenet dynasty

Now that she had accomplished her mission, Eleanor permanently retired to Fontevraud (just like her daughter Joan had done a short while before her death) to become a nun. News of the capture of Château-Gaillard (Eure), on the 6th of March 1204, was brought to her, putting an end to any ambition for the Plantagenet's supremacy over the continent. Exhausted by a life of incessant combat, Eleanor, in turn, passed away three weeks later – on the 31st of March 1204 – at the age of eighty. She was buried in the abbey-church, donning a simple nun's clothing, next to her husband. Eleanor's grave was desecrated during the French Revolution and her bones were scattered. All that remains is her recumbent polychrome stone statue, where she is depicted holding a book in her hand. The Counts of Anjou left their mark on the history of this abbey, founded in 1101 by Robert of Arbrissel. From Fulk V, King of Jerusalem, to Eleanor, they all strove to superbly adorn the site, of which they were unanimously fond. Most of these illustrious figures are laid to rest there: Henry II (1189), Richard the Lionheart and his sister Joan (1199), Eleanor of Aquitaine (1204). Later, in 1246, the sepulchre of John Lackland's wife, Isabella of Angoulême, joined those of the Plantagenets.

Detail of the recumbent statue of Henry II Plantagenet, Abbey of Fontevraud.

Recumbent statues of Isabella of Angoulême and Richard the Lionheart, Abbey of Fontevraud.

Fontevraud abbey-church (Maine-et-Loire).

Comparative family trees of Louis VII and Eleanor of Aquitaine

These comparative family trees highlight the relationships between Louis VII and Eleanor that served as grounds for the annulment of their marriage. We can nevertheless note that similar family links existed between Eleanor and Henry Plantagenet, who descended from Rollo on his mother's side, without any such links calling their union into question.

Louis VII's ancestors

Robert the Strong
(deceased in 866), Count of Anjou

Robert I,
King of France (circa 922-933),
spouse Beatrice of Vermandois

Hugh the Great,
Duke of France (deceased in 956),
spouse Hedwig of Saxony

Hugh Capet,
King of France (979-996), spouse Adelaide of Aquitaine,
daughter of William Towhead and **Gerloc/Adele.**

Robert II the Pious,
King of France (996-1031),
spouse Constance of Arles

Henry I,
King of France (1031-1060,
spouse Anne of Kiev

Philip I,
King of France (1060-1108),
spouse Bertha of Holland

Louis VI the Fat,
King of France (1108-1137),
spouse Adelaide of Savoy

Louis VII the Young

Eleanor's ancestors

Gerard, Count of Auvergne
(deceased in 841)

Ranulf I of Poitiers,
Duke of Aquitaine (deceased in 867)

Ranulf II of Poitiers,
Duke of Aquitaine (deceased in 890)

Ebalus Manzer,
Count of Poitiers (deceased in 935)

William III of Poitiers,
'Towhead' (abdicated in 963),
spouse **Gerloc/Adele, daughter of Rollo**

William IV 'Fierebras',
Count of Poitiers, Duke of Aquitaine (963-995),
spouse Emma of Blois

William V the Great,
Count of Poitiers, Duke of Aquitaine (995-1030),
spouse Agnes of Burgundy

William VIII,
Count of Poitiers, Duke of Aquitaine (1058-1086),
reigned with his half-brother William VI
and his brother William VII,
spouse, Hildegarde of Burgundy

William IX the Troubador,
Count of Poitiers, Duke of Aquitaine
(1086-1126 or 1127),
spouse Philippa, Countess of Toulouse

William X,
Count of Poitiers, Duke of Aquitaine (1126 or 1127-1137),
spouse Aénor of Châtellerault

Eleanor of Aquitaine

Eleanor's children

With Louis VII

- Marie (1145-1198), spouse of Henry I, Count of Champagne
- Alix (1151-after 1198), spouse of Thibaut, Count of Blois

With Henry II

- William (1153-1156)
- Henry the Young King (1155-1183), King of England
- Matilda (1156-1189), spouse of Henry the Lion, Duke of Bavaria
- Richard I, the Lionheart (1157-1199), King of England, Duke of Normandy, Duke of Aquitaine, Count of Poitiers, Count of Maine, Count of Anjou
- Geoffrey (1158-1186), Duke of Brittany in 1169
- Eleanor (1162-1214), spouse of Alfonso VIII, King of Castile, mother to (among others) Blanche of Castile, future Queen of France.
- Joan (1165-1199), spouse of William II, King of Sicily, then of Raymond VI, Count of Toulouse
- John Lackland (1166-1216), King of England

Bibliography

CHAUOU (Amaury), *Sur les pas d'Aliénor d'Aquitaine*, Editions Ouest-France, 2005.

DELORME (Philippe), *Aliénor d'Aquitaine*, Pygmalion, 2013.

DELVAILLE (Bernard), *Mille et cent ans de poésie française*, Bouquins, Robert Laffont, 1991.

FLORI (Jean), *Aliénor d'Aquitaine, la Reine insoumise*, Payot, 2004.

HIVERGNEAUX (Marie), 'Aliénor d'Aquitaine: le pouvoir d'une femme à là lumière de ses chartes – 1152-1204', interview published in *L'Actualité Poitou-Charentes* n°65, 2004.

PERNOUD (Régine), *Aliénor d'Aquitaine*, Albin Michel, 1965, new edition published by Livre de Poche, 1983.

RICHARD (Jean), *Histoire des croisades*, Fayard, 1996.

TURNER (Ralph V.), *Aliénor d'Aquitaine*, Fayard, 2011. (Translated from English)

Detail of the stained-glass window representing Eleanor and Henry II of England, Cathedral of Saint Peter of Poitiers.

OREP
EDITIONS

Zone Tertiaire de NONANT - 14400 BAYEUX
Tel: 02 31 51 81 31 - Fax: 02 31 51 81 32 - E-mail: info@orepeditions.com - Web: www.orepeditions.com
Editor: Grégory Pique - Editorial Coordination: Sophie Lajoye – Translation: Heather Inglis.
Proof-reading: Roger Jouet
ISBN: 978-2-8151-0398-5 - Copyright OREP 2017 – Legal deposit: 1st quarter 2020